Guess a Rhyme

Hop, jump, run,

Riddle-dee-rhyme fun!

A Random House PICTUREBACK®

a Rhyme

RIDDLES TO SOLVE!

by Larry Weinberg   illustrated by Roy McKie

You can rhyme.

Just take a LOOK!

Answer: look

Random House New York

Text Copyright © 1982 by Larry Weinberg. Illustrations Copyright © 1982 by Random House, Inc. All rights reserved under International and Pan-American Copyright Conventions. Published in the United States by Random House, Inc., New York, and simultaneously in Canada by Random House of Canada Limited, Toronto. *Library of Congress Cataloging in Publication Data:* Weinberg, Larry. Guess a rhyme. (Pictureback) SUMMARY: A collection of poems with final rhyming words omitted, allowing the reader to guess the correct word to complete each poem. 1. Children's poetry, American. [I. American poetry. 2. English language—Rhyme. 3. Literary recreations] I. Title. PS3573.E3918G8 811'.54 81-15689 AACR2 ISBN: 0-394-85062-9 Manufactured in the United States of America 1 2 3 4 5 6 7 8 9 0

They came to our picnic!

Acted very rude!

Came uninvited,

Gobbled up our food!

They crawled on our blanket,

Our ankles and our pants!

Call that a picnic?

Yes, for the __ __ __ __!

Answer: ants

Witches and goblins

and vampire bats

Can only scare

the scaredy __ __ __ __!

Answer: cats

The mice were gathered in a crowd,

That is, until the cat ___ ___ ___ ___ ___ ___.

Answer: meowed

At jumping I am
The greatest of all.

In winter I spring!
In summer I ___ ___ ___ ___!

Answer: fall

The gardener had a birthday.

The baker made a cake.

He put in lots of fallen leaves

And then threw in the rake.

He covered it with mud and twigs

And baked it with delight.

The cake was very nice to see

But no one took a __ __ __ __!

Answer: bite

I have a boat

That I often _ _ _ _ _

To the other end of me.

My bar of soap

Is the sailing boat,

My bathtub is the _ _ _ _.

Answers: float sea

If you enjoy the
wind that blows,
winter snows,
frozen toes,
Then you could live with
_ _ _ _ _ _ _ _!

Answer: Eskimos

I wrote a letter
To an Irish setter,
But he thought it was a bone.
He chewed up
Every word of it.
Next time I'll use the _ _ _ _ _.

Answer: phone

What has four legs and a long tail
and can't neigh anymore?
A hoarse __ __ __ __ __.

Answer: a hoarse horse

When I was one
My sister was two.
When I was three
My sister was four.
When I was five
My sister was six.
Now I am seven
And going on eight.
Won't someone please tell
My sister to __ __ __ __!

Answer: wait

"Where did you put the cherries, George,
After you chopped the tree?"

"Father, I put them in a pie
And put the pie in __ __."

"Son, I'm glad you did not lie
And now take my advice:
Next time you do a thing like that
Please save your dad a __ __ __ __ __!"

A school of fish
Is not a class.
It's just a large collection
Of many fish
With a similar wish
To go in one __ __ __ __ __ __ __ __ __.

A pair of shoes
Are on the street
And in the shoes
Are my two _ _ _ _ _ .

Where they walk
No one knows,
Except myself
And my ten _ _ _ _ _ .

Answers: feet toes

Down in the bottom
Of a deep dark well
The Cat in the Hat
And the Lorax dwell,
Waiting 'til they are
Put to use
In another great book
By Doctor _ _ _ _ _ _ !

Answer: Seuss

When you reach the age of ten

Would you like to start again?

Be one year old

And then be two,

Do all the things you used to __ __?

Live in diapers,

Lie in a crib,

Get powdered all over

And wear a __ __ __?

Maybe YOU would like that fine

But I don't think I have the __ __ __ __!

Lots and lots and lots
    of fishes
Thought that Jonah
    looked delicious.
Good to eat with
    pepper and salt,
Good to mix in a
    chocolate _ _ _ _ _,
Good to pop in an
    ice cream cone,
Good to nibble
    all alone.
But only one that thought him
    yummy
Got Jonah down inside its

    _ _ _ _ _ _.

Answers: malt tummy

I have a kid sister named Daisy,
She never is messy or lazy.
She does everything right
From morning 'til _ _ _ _ _.
She's purposely driving me _ _ _ _ _!

Answers: night   crazy

What is a very small hot dog?
A teenie _ _ _ _ _ _.

Answer: a teenie weenie

My birthday was full
Of some awful surprises!
No toys! Only clothes!
And in the wrong _ _ _ _ _ _!

Answer: sizes

I went to the kitchen
To take a little drink,
But I stopped with surprise
When I saw the kitchen _ _ _ _!

Answer: sink

Merlin got his magic power
By eating almost every hour.
Just in case you'd care to try it,
Here is Merlin's magic diet:

Old maps,
Bottle _ _ _ _ _ .

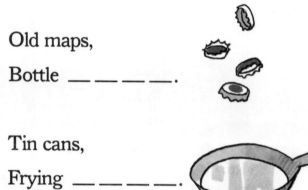

Tin cans,
Frying _ _ _ _ _ .

Dumbbells,
Ink _ _ _ _ _ _ .

China plates,
Roller _ _ _ _ _ _ _ .

Woolen socks,
Building _ _ _ _ _ _ _ .

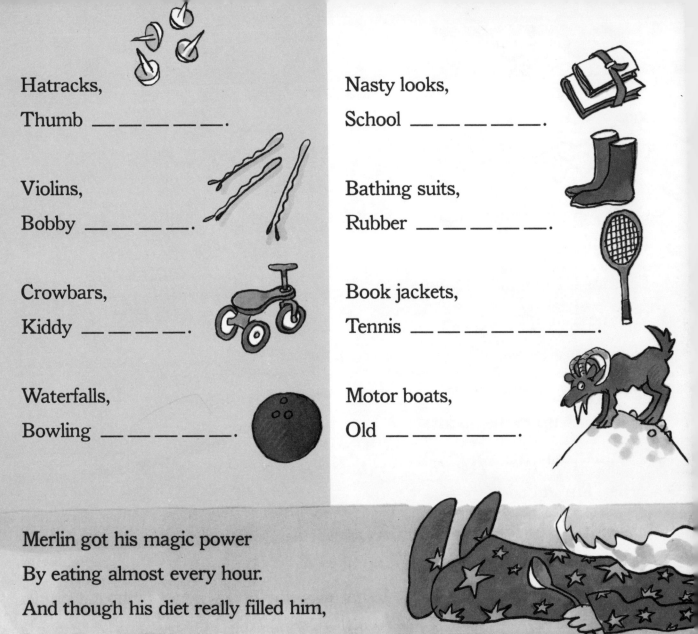

Hatracks,
Thumb _ _ _ _ _.

Nasty looks,
School _ _ _ _ _.

Violins,
Bobby _ _ _ _ _.

Bathing suits,
Rubber _ _ _ _ _.

Crowbars,
Kiddy _ _ _ _.

Book jackets,
Tennis _ _ _ _ _ _.

Waterfalls,
Bowling _ _ _ _ _.

Motor boats,
Old _ _ _ _ _.

Merlin got his magic power
By eating almost every hour.
And though his diet really filled him,
It's sad to say it also _ _ _ _ _ _ _ _.

Can't I stay up and watch this show?

It's really a good story.

I promise I will hide my eyes

Whenever it gets gory.

I'll stuff my ears

When the monster roars

And beats upon the door.

It won't scare me

When I'm in bed—

I've seen it twice __ __ __ __ __ __ !

Answer: before

What was the kitty when a hippo sat on her?

A flat __ __ __ .

Answer: a flat cat

What was Smokey when he lost his fur?

A bare __ __ __ __ .

Here I am
In my cage in the zoo.
I swing by my tail
But I'm a lot like __ __ __ !

So don't jabber, jabber
Or climb a tree
Or make monkey faces
Just like __ __ .

'Cause if you do
The things I do
They might put YOU
In the __ __ __ !

"He hit me hard.
That's why I'm crying!"

"She pushed me first.
She's lying, she's lying!"

"He yelled at me.
That's why I did it!"

"She took my football
And she ___ ___ ___ it!"

"That's because he
Called me dumb!"

"I said it 'cause she
Bit my ___ ___ ___ ___ ___!"

"Children! Children!
For goodness' sake,
Give your mother
And me a ___ ___ ___ ___ ___!"

On Naughtiness Day

You can really be bad.

You can make your mother awfully _ _ _.

You can tease your brother

And your sister too.

You can holler and scream

'Til your face is _ _ _ _.

You can go to the table

With a dirty face

And take a seat

That's not your place.

You can feed the dog

What you don't like,

Go out and ride

Your brother's _ _ _ _.

But one thing should be understood:

The rest of the year

You must be _ _ _ _.

Every day I feed a carrot

To my favorite green _ _ _ _ _ _ _.

Today she squawked, "Please break the habit

Or get yourself a dumb white _ _ _ _ _ _ _."

Answers: parrot rabbit

What did King Arthur wear when he went to bed?

A knight's _ _ _ _ _ _ _ _.

Answer: a knight's nightie

The equator runs around the earth.
It runs and runs for all it's worth.

It cannot stop to rest its feet.
It cannot even stop to eat.
It cannot stop to change its clothes.
It cannot even blow its _ _ _ _ _.
It cannot stop to see a show.
It cannot even say _ _ _ _ _.
It cannot stop to read a book.
It cannot even stop to _ _ _ _.

The equator runs with all it's got.
No wonder that it gets so _ _ _!

Answers: nose hello look hot

"You dare to serve on *paper* plates!
And here I am, the Queen!"
  "Your Majesty, the whole world says
  They keep the palace clean."

"Why do you bring me soda pop
When I drink only wine?"
  "Your Majesty, the whole world says
  Pop makes the party shine."

"And what about this candy bar
When I am on a diet?"
  "Your Majesty, the whole world says
  You really ought to ____ ___."

"And where's my gold and ruby crown
That goes upon my head?"
  "Your Majesty, the whole world says
  To try this cap instead."

"But that's a hat that has a point.
They put it on a dunce!"
  "Your Majesty, the whole world says
  You ought to try it ___ ___ ___ ___."

"But won't they say I am a fool
To wear this on my brow?"
  "Your Majesty, the whole world says
  That's what you are right ___ ___ ___."

Answers: try it once now

Stick your face
Up close to mine
And look into my eyes.
Now I have you
In my power,
I can _ _ _ _ _ _ _ _ _ _ _.
You are tired,
            tired,
            tired.
You're getting sleepy too.
Sleepy, sleepy, sleepy—
There's nothing you can do,
You'll soon be dreaming,
                dreaming,
                dreaming
For you are in my power.

And now, dear Mommy,
YOU go to bed
And I'll stay up an _ _ _ _!

Answer: hypnotize hour.

Mr. and Mrs. *I Don't Know*
Named their son *I Told You So.*
He grew up and married *I Don't Care*
And went to live in *Who Knows Where.*
That's in the State of *Can't You See*
And there they raised a *Don't Blame* __ __!

Answer: *Me*

Were you ever told
To "hold your tongue"?
That's hard to do
When you are young.
You have to open
Up real wide
To get your fingers
Down inside.
Besides, a tongue
Is very wet
And all the words
May slip out __ __ __.

Answer: yet

Have you ever heard of Opposite Day

When everything works the other way?

When "good" means "bad"
And "right" means "wrong."
"Night" is "day"
And "short" is " _ _ _ _ _."

"Up" is "down"
And "in" is "out."
And "stop!" means "go!"
And "shush!" means " _ _ _ _ _ _!"

"I want it" means

"I really don't."

"I'll do it" means

"I really __ __ __ __."

"I'm hungry" means

"I'm really not."

"It's cold in here" means

"It's too __ __ __!"

And "Yes, I am a sleepy head"

Means "I'm not ready yet for __ __ __!"

Well, that's the way you have to play

When all night long it's Opposite __ __ __!

The king was neither short nor tall,
He wasn't fat or lean.
And though he wasn't very nice
He wasn't very mean.

It's true he wasn't very smart,
But then, he wasn't dumb.
And though he hated lollipops
He loved to suck his ＿＿＿＿＿.

He wasn't much at working hard,
But then, he wasn't lazy.
And though his head was not quite right
He really wasn't ＿＿＿＿＿.

He wasn't the very, very best
Nor the worst that could have been.
But just the sort of king to have
In the Land of In-Be ＿＿＿＿＿.

Every single tooth extraction

Is a lesson in sub __ __ __ __ __ __ __ __ __ __.

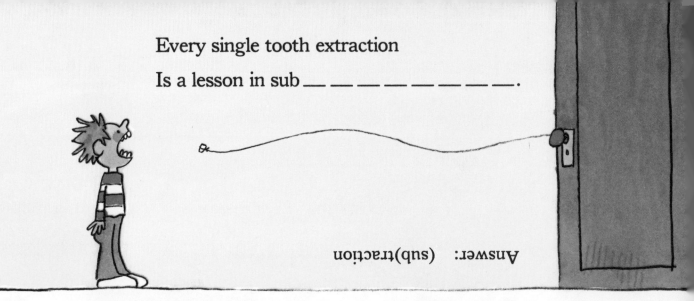

I'm never mean,

I never get mad.

I'm never naughty

And never __ __ __.

I'm never wrong

And I'm always right.

I never fib

And I never __ __ __ __ __.

If you believe

This song is true,

There must be something

__ __ __ __ __ with you!

The ice cream man,

That crazy man,

He threw the cones

In the garbage __ __ __.

He threw the ice cream

In the lake,

He threw away

The ice cream __ __ __ __.

He threw the sprinkles

In the air

And down they came

I don't know __ __ __ __ __.

The cherries I love

He also threw.

It drove me NUTS—

And he threw those __ __ __!